D0112431

Living in Joyful Hope

Advent and Christmas Meditations

Suzanne M. Lewis

**Catechesis of
the Good Shepherd
Publications**

LIVING IN JOYFUL HOPE: ADVENT AND CHRISTMAS MEDITATIONS © 2005 Archdiocese of Chicago: Liturgy Training Publications, 1800 North Hermitage Avenue, Chicago IL 60622-1101; 1-800-933-1800, fax 1-800-933-7094, e-mail orders@ltp.org. All rights reserved. See our website at www.ltp.org.

Catechesis of the Good Shepherd Publications is an imprint of Liturgy Training Publications (LTP). Further information about these publications is available from LTP or from the Catechesis of the Good Shepherd, PO Box 1084, Oak Park IL 60304; 708-542-1210; fax 708-386-8032. Requests for information about other aspects of the Catechesis should be directed to this address.

Other Catechesis of the Good Shepherd Books Include
The Religious Potential of the Child, Sofia Cavalletti
The Religious Potential of the Child 6 to 12 Years Old, Sofia Cavalletti
Living Liturgy, Sofia Cavalletti
History's Golden Thread, Sofia Cavalletti
The Good Shepherd and the Child: A Joyful Journey, Patricia Coulter, Silvana Montenarro, and Sofia Cavalletti
Essential Realities, Tina Lillig, ed.
A is for Altar, B is for Bible, Judy Main
The Catechesis of the Good Shepherd in a Parish Setting, Tina Lillig
Mustard Seed Preaching, Ann Garrido

This book was edited by Danielle A. Knott. Carol Mycio was the production editor. The design is by Anna Manhart, and the typesetting was done by Kari Nicholls in Bembo and Optima. The art is by Kathy Ann Sullivan.

Printed in the United States of America.

Library of Congress Control Number: 2005929208

ISBN 1-56854-590-8

CGSJH

This book is dedicated to:

Stephan

Sophie

Simone

Serena

Sylvie

and

Stella

with all my love

Contents

Introduction

During Advent and Christmas we await and celebrate the birth of Christ in order to tune our hearts to await and celebrate the fulfillment of God's "plan for the fullness of time, to gather up all things in Christ, things in heaven and things on earth" (Ephesians 1:10). What better way to tune our hearts than by listening, with great care and attention, to the word of God? In this book, I hope that the short verses from the Bible, and the reflections and prayers that follow, can serve as a springboard to your personal reflection on the word of God. May we have a holy and joyful Advent and Christmas.

Let the children be our models. We will savor every sacred word from scripture, and in joy, our hope will blossom in the Light that has been born in our midst. Amen.

Acknowledgment

The meditations in this book are the fruit of a completely new experience of the church that I had in October of 1997. Up until that moment, my religious life had been hidden in my heart, a treasure that was formless and almost impossible to communicate. What little of it that I could put into words, I had shared with those I love. But the most beautiful things, the richest and most precious realities, seemed beyond the reach of words. Thus, I could only contemplate them in solitude and with a very dim understanding.

I had read Teresa of Avila and T. S. Eliot and sayings of the Desert Fathers and Thomas Merton and of course, the Bible. Words jounced around in my head, but in my own mouth, they seemed like cracked vessels, never capable of containing the most important things in my heart.

Then, in October of 1997, when I walked into my first atrium to drop off my oldest child for her Catechesis of the Good Shepherd session, I met up with a new and utterly surprising means of religious expression: Holy Simplicity.

Was it in the songs, so beautiful and full of dignity, when the children sang together? Or perhaps, as I glanced about the room, the order and scope and sobriety of the hand-made materials wakened something in me? Maybe the catechist's words, so carefully chosen and full of curiosity and wonder, opened a door? All these things may be true, but what struck me on that day were the children themselves, so serious and thoughtful and hungry for these great realities presented to them without embellishment or apology. The reverence and awe of the children seemed to match up with that secret, wordless experience I had only had in solitude. They were absorbed, thoughtful, and certain as they listened and spoke about hidden, precious, tiny, and mysterious realities that open out on the vastness of the divine life.

From that day, I began to attend sessions along with my children, and eventually I became a catechist.

This book is the result of many hours spent listening to God with children. Out of this experience, I began a journey that led me beyond the atrium, to joyful hours alone with the word of God; to a deepening satisfaction and pleasure in participation in the Mass; to the beautiful writings of Sofia Cavalletti, Gianna Gobbi, Maria Montessori, and their collaborators; to the authors Sofia cites in her bibliographies and footnotes; as well as to the counsel and example and great friendship of other catechists who have fallen in love with the Good Shepherd.

In fact, those who are familiar with the writings of Sofia Cavalletti don't need to be told that her insights and discoveries occur on every page of this book. It would be impossible to footnote every place where her thought has influenced my own. The book would consist mostly of footnotes! Besides, I myself do not always recognize when I am using her original thoughts. They have become a part of the way I view and understand the world. I can only gratefully acknowledge her wisdom and scholarship.

Each meditation in this book begins with a verse or two from the Bible; as Sofia so often remarks, "the initiative is always God's."

These verses come from presentations that we explore with children in the Catechesis of the Good Shepherd. While the meditations reflect my own adult thoughts and experiences, they are completely dependent on the many hours spent with the children and in close study of Sofia's and Gianna's work. Thus, like all of God's gifts, they are mine yet not mine. I offer them with deep and abiding gratitude to the "mothers" of the Catechesis and to all, particularly the children, who have prayed and probed these mysteries with me. Any grace they contain comes from them; the misapprehensions are all mine.

A Note to Catechists

The Catechesis of the Good Shepherd seeks to allow children to explore God's mysteries at their own pace. We begin with the Bible and with elements of liturgy, and with great patience and *restraint*, we provide the conditions under which the children may discover connections and theological insights for themselves. We must never spoil their enjoyment by attempting to impose on them our own discoveries and insights. We must remember that our job is to proclaim the *kerygma* (the preaching of the Gospel) without embellishment. It requires true faith to know when to remain silent and allow the word of God to work unimpeded in the hearts of God's children.

Thus, the meditations in this book are not intended for use with children. They are personal reflections on the scriptures. By sharing them with you, I hope to invite you to enjoy these readings and to inspire you to continue to mine their bottomless depth.

The Season
of Advent

Isaiah's Prophecy of the Light

༺

Isaiah 9:2

Reading

The people who walked in darkness
have seen a great light.

Isaiah 9:2

Reflection

Each minute of sunlight feels so precious in these darkest weeks of winter. We, like sunflowers, seem to draw vital energy from our bright star. Like morning glories, we open wide to its warmth and light.

How is the light of the Good Shepherd different from sunlight?

What a light he is! So glorious and great, and yet his light never injures. We will never have too much of this tremendous vitality. His light remains in me, even as I am enveloped in his inflaming joy.

I received his beautiful light as a gift. I did not merit this gift. I did not even know how to ask for so glorious a gift. And my gratitude will never be equal to it.

There have been times when the dark days of winter have frightened and discouraged me. I have sometimes forgotten that in truth, nothing can hide the marvelous light of the Good Shepherd, nothing can stand between me and his great light. At every moment, he calls to me. I only need to turn my face to him. I need only to open my heart, wider each day, until that day when all hearts will be opened.

The light of the Good Shepherd is more solid, more dependable than any object found in the physical world. When we lean against it, it bears all our weight. And when we abandon ourselves to it completely, it will lift us up.

Prayer

Your word is a lamp to my feet
  and a light to my path.
Your decrees are my heritage forever;
  they are the joy of my heart.
The unfolding of your words gives light;
  it imparts understanding to the simple.

Psalm 119:105, 111, 130

hen all around me is darkness, O Lord,
I turn to your word. I open
my heart to your ancient teaching,
  to the sacred mystery of your scripture.
One verse from the Bible imparts
joy beyond all telling. I will turn
again and read of how you commanded
the light to *be* light.
I will arise;
my own light will shine
because your Word is within me.
One day your Word will overtake the world
completely.
What a light it will be
when all have arisen
and all shine with your glory!
Amen.

The Annunciation
of the Lord

❧

Luke 1:26–38

Reading

In the sixth month the angel Gabriel was sent by God to a town in Galilee called Nazareth, to a virgin engaged to a man whose name was Joseph, of the house of David. The virgin's name was Mary.

Luke 1:26–27

Reflection

"In the sixth month . . ." at a very particular time, "to a town in Galilee called Nazareth . . ." in a particular place, God intervened in our history. God created time but lives in the ageless eternity of wonder. Our God sanctified time and made of it a tabernacle where he might be forever revealed. God, whose omnipresence transcends all points of the compass, took sanctuary in a town, thereby making of town life something both awesome and holy. God will not even be confined by limitless possibility! God reached across the chasm that separates us from transcendence so that we who inhabit our own historical moment, our own towns, may live richly, full of grace now, here. Through God's gift of himself, our now becomes forever, and we can touch that moment when time will cease to exist.

And he didn't simply enter time and space; he approached a person, with a name, Mary. Mary becomes the living tabernacle and sanctuary of the Lord. From this day, flesh itself is transformed into the holiest dwelling place of the Most High.

Prayer

See the place where God lives among his people; there the Spirit
of God will make his home among you; the temple of God is holy
and you are that temple.

From the Rite of Dedication of a Church, 64

 God, my God, I have looked upon you in the
sanctuary—
how often have I looked upon you in the sanctuary!
You do live among your people,
you do make your home among us.
When I behold my brothers and sisters,
your face shines from their features, your hands
grasp mine when they reach to me
offering your peace, asking your forgiveness.
What a responsibility you have given me,
to be your eyes, your lips, your hands!
You invite me to pay attention
to what you do now, with my own hands, with the
hands of strangers, outcasts, the friendless, children.
Your marvels are everywhere!
How you honor me!
Today,
it takes my breath away to say it,
everywhere I gaze, I may look upon you.
Wherever I reach, with these very hands,
you touch
the universe.
Amen.

Reading

And he came to her and said, "Greetings. . . ."

Luke 1:28a

Reflection

In the Greek New Testament, Gabriel's word of greeting is *"Chaire,"* which literally means, "Rejoice!"

In fact, Gabriel calls all of us to rejoice with Mary. No matter our life situation, as Christians, our first vocation is *to rejoice.*

But can we aspire to joy? Can we earn it? Do we need a special talent or vocation to attain it?

On the brief occasions when we do experience joy, we are almost always surprised, or even shocked, into it. For this reason, joy seems to come more easily to children—for them so much of life is new and surprising. But by the time we reach adulthood, even the experience of being surprised can seem to be routine.

What if we were to recognize that so much of what we have and touch is ultimately mysterious? We never did hope for the physical world to include colors—or for the ability to see them. We never could have dreamed of the existence of music—or invented a means to hear it. Though we might earn our bread, the earth produced wheat before any human hand existed to reap, thresh, mill, mix, or bake it into a loaf.

When we allow ourselves to be astonished by the seemingly ordinary, then each glance, each overheard note, each morsel of bread becomes an occasion for wonder and joy!

Rejoice!

And if we recognize that the ordinary has the power to astonish, what will happen when we contemplate the birth of Jesus of Nazareth?

Everything—or rather *more* than everything—became a something, *one* thing, a human being.

Expression itself became an expression.

The Architect of the cosmos became one frail and vulnerable element in his own vast structure (the dimensions of which we could never measure!).

Perfect Love desires our puny, stumbling love.

Joy invites us to participate with our own imperfect joy in the divine life.

Pondering these truths in our hearts, *how can we escape astonishment?*

Prayer

Rejoice in the LORD, O you righteous.
   Praise befits the upright.
Praise the LORD with the lyre;
   make melody to him with the harp of ten strings.
Sing to him a new song;
   play skillfully on the strings, with loud shouts.

Psalm 33:1–3

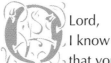Lord,
   I know
   that you rejoice
      in the work of your hands.
      When I work with my own hands
      please let me fill the world
      with the glorious melody
      that I become when you touch
      the ten strings
      of my heart.
      Let others join this heavenly music,
      until that day when the whole world is filled
      with your song.
      Amen.

Reading

And he came to her and said, "Greetings, favored one! The Lord is with you." But she was much perplexed by his words and pondered what sort of greeting this might be.

Luke 1:28–29

Reflection

What was it that so perplexed Mary? Instead of using her name, Gabriel gave her a title, a most strange and perplexing title for an ordinary peasant girl living in a town of no consequence: *"kecharitomene."* Sometimes translated as "favored" or "full of grace," *"kecharitomene"* is more accurately translated: "You who have been and are now filled with divine favor."

No one in the whole history of salvation, no one except Mary, has been greeted this way by an angel.

We often say that Mary was "without sin," describing her by what she was *without;* when in fact, Mary's great distinguishing characteristic, the prerequisite for all the glory that followed, is that Mary was, and still is, radically *with:* even before she was with child, she was with the Lord, and the Lord was with her. She was full, brimming, already, in some mysterious way, pregnant with our Lord, who is all grace and all favor.

But what amazes us, knowing what we know of Mary's destiny, is that she did not seem to *know* that the divine life had filled her. She was perplexed and pondered what the angel's greeting could mean.

God resides with us in silence, in stillness, in our openness, and in our desire for meaning; the Spirit enters us, not when we're blowing out hot air, but when we breathe in. Vanity turns us toward a mirror hung in a room sized only to our own dimensions and away from the window that opens out into the fresh air and limitless horizons of divine life.

God waits so patiently for us to turn again, to come to our senses, to open our eyes and ears, to breathe the breath of life, to open our hands and mouths to receive his grace, to *taste* his goodness, to be "*kecharitomene,*" and never to stop pondering the glorious announcement that Emmanuel has heard our desperate cry. He has already come. He will always be with us, until the end of time.

Prayer

You have ravished my heart, my sister, my bride,
   you have ravished my heart with a glance of your eyes,
   with one jewel of your necklace.
How sweet is your love, my sister, my bride!
   how much better is your love than wine,
   and the fragrance of your oils than any spice!

Song of Solomon 4:9–10

earest Jesus,
   when you came to your mother,
   it was with all the passion of a bridegroom
   drunk with love. When you approach
   me, you come not with arguments and definitions,
   but to *entice.*
   Your love is sweet, better than any wine.
   You invite me to drink, to taste you,
   to breathe in the fragrance of your holy joy
   because for you I am—
   I am astonished every time I think it—
   beloved.
   Amen.

Reading

The angel said to her, "Do not be afraid, Mary, for you have found favor with God. And now, you will conceive in your womb and bear a son, and you will name him Jesus. He will be great, and will be called the Son of the Most High, and the Lord God will give to him the throne of his ancestor David. He will reign over the house of Jacob forever, and of his kingdom there will be no end."

Luke 1:30–33

Reflection

Gabriel begins by saying that Mary's son will be "great." Then he improves on that idea by announcing that Jesus will be called "the Son of the Most High." Gabriel's words build momentum, stacking glory upon glory. By the internal logic of the angel's syntax, the next thing said about Jesus should be even more wonderful. Thus, when God gives Jesus the "throne" of David, we know to seek for the divine meaning in this regal image.

Perhaps a key to understanding this "throne" lies in the psalms of David. These songs of faithful adherence, of supplication and praise, breathe with divine life. When the psalms exhale, adoration, wonder, and awe rise like incense into the heavens. When they reflect on the mighty deeds and tender compassion of our Lord, the psalms inhale the very substance of God. David's throne of words is a holy and living seat within the Bible, which is itself a palace that contains the eternal Word. When we pray, we curl up on God's lap; we share the throne of David and we abide in eternity.

While Jesus walked the earth, he embodied divine mercy, justice, and love with each breath he took; as the ever-living Word of God, Jesus incarnates the very breath of God. This breath will fill the universe with warmth and will vivify the cosmos.

The throne of David furnishes the tabernacle of love. Upon this throne sits the very soul of prayer.

Prayer

You prepare a table before me
   in the presence of my enemies;
you anoint my head with oil;
   my cup overflows.
Surely goodness and mercy shall follow me
   all the days of my life,
and I shall dwell in the house of the LORD
   my whole life long.

   Psalm 23:5–6

y Good Shepherd,
   God's anointed,
      my king and my God,
   your table and your throne
   are one and the same.
   I want only to live and abide
   in your holy dwelling,
   to drink from the overflowing cup
   of your word,
   sweeter than honey,
   and your Word, broken
   and shared.
   Open my lips,
   find sanctuary in me,
   and I will sing your praise
   all the days of my life.
   Amen.

Reading

Mary said to the angel, "How can this be, since I am a virgin?"

Luke 1:34

Reflection

Mary dared to question an angel!

Six months earlier, when Gabriel announced to Zechariah that his wife, Elizabeth, would conceive and bear a child, Zechariah asked, "How will I know that this is so?" As a result, the angel punished Zechariah for doubting.

How is Mary's question different from Zechariah's?

Mary's question was *quiet*. She simply asked for understanding.

Zechariah's question betrayed a desire for proof: "How will I know?" He wanted to gather the evidence and then render a decision, *his* decision. This attitude locked Zechariah within the limited sphere of what he could know. He could not make room for the marvelous. His punishment manifested his condition: no longer able to speak, his thoughts and desires became closed up inside of him.

By contrast, Mary's question, full of wonder, indicated that she was open, so wide open that the eternal Son of the Most High would take up residence *in her body*.

Still, we may wonder why Mary would ask a question at this moment.

Where did Mary's desire for knowledge come from? What does her desire signify?

If once we have received a real taste of the sacred, we become hungry for more. Our small awareness leads us to recognize how scant, how provisional, how circumscribed we are. And though limited, we thirst to be complete. To live with this sense of lack is part of our human condition. To meet this need becomes our quest.

Our hunger, though often painful, is a tremendous gift. It animates and energizes us for all the work the Spirit invites us to do. Our hunger impels us to seek the Eternal.

If we can honestly and bravely face the truth of our finitude, even while refusing to abandon our conviction that there must be a response to our deepest need, we will soon discover an interior door. This door opens onto a world of wonder. With hearts open, we will be propelled on a journey to seek everywhere, and in every person we meet, after the face of God. We will find God in the most unlikely, most humble and ordinary places! And on that day, we will have all we need.

Prayer

If you indeed cry out for insight,
    and raise your voice for understanding;
if you seek it like silver,
    and search for it as for hidden treasures—
then you will understand the fear of the LORD
    and find the knowledge of God.

Proverbs 2:3–5

ear God,
Mary's whole life sounds
    a single pure note,
    perfectly in tune
    with your plan.
    Like Mary, I will listen for the music of your joy
    with my whole self.
    My only wish is to place myself in your hands
    so that you can make me vibrate,
    like Mary,
    one with you.
    Amen.

Reading

The angel said to her, "The Holy Spirit will come upon you. . . .

Luke 1:35a

Reflection

Wings spread, hovering in the air, rays of gold emanate from the dove's body, bathing Mary in a shower of light.

A dove once flew across the dark waters of the flood. Under those waters, every living thing had been blotted out: "Everything on dry land in whose nostrils was the breath of life died" (Genesis 7:22). The very essence of life that God had once breathed directly into Adam's nostrils was quenched beneath the waves. The dove soared over these lifeless waters and returned to Noah in the evening, with a freshly plucked olive leaf in its beak.

In the early Church, the Tree of Life in the Garden of Eden was thought by some to be an olive tree. Oil pressed from its fruit anoints priests, prophets, and kings. The Messiah, the Christ, the One who was to come, is "God's anointed." He is the new shoot that sprouts from a dead stump, the Tree of Life transplanted from the center of the Garden of Eden, to the center of our hearts.

Here is the olive branch, flourishing in the midst of a world suffocating in sin. Here is the fresh balm that will heal and perfume the cosmos. To a young girl, whose innermost self will open out to the wonders of the Lord, the dove bears this green shoot: a baby, the Prince of Peace.

Prayer

After the avenging flood,
the dove returning to Noah with an olive branch
announced your gift of peace.
This was a sign of a greater gift to come.
Now the waters of baptism wash away the sins of men,
and by the anointing with olive oil
you make us radiant with your joy.

From the Rite of Consecration of the Chrism, 25

ome, Holy Spirit, come:
heal me with your balm,
refine my heart in the fire of your love,
help me to soar with your wings,
enliven me with your gladness,
make me radiant with your joy.
Come, Holy Spirit, come:
let me exude the fragrance of Christ,
that my prayer might be acceptable to God.
Amen.

Reading

. . . .And the power of the Most High will overshadow you; therefore the child to be born will be holy; he will be called Son of God. . . .

Luke 1:35b

Reflection

How often the power of the Most High, manifested as a bright cloud, overshadowed the tent of meeting that Moses had erected in the desert! Moses had furnished the tent, according to God's own command; in the heart of the tent, in the holy of holies, God commanded that Moses place an ark to house the covenant. The ark was made of pure gold. Two cherubim of pure gold were fashioned of hammered gold "of a piece" with the gold "mercy seat" or cover for the ark. God commanded that "the cherubim shall spread out their wings above, overshadowing the mercy seat with their wings" (Exodus 25:20).

During those times when the bright cloud settled upon the tent, Moses was not able to enter it, because the glory of the Lord filled the tabernacle.

Yet Gabriel announces that the power of the Most High will now overshadow a person, an unremarkable girl! The angel had told her not to fear. But these must have been fearsome words. What did Mary think?

We must also ask, did the angel's answer to Mary's question bring clarity? The event Gabriel heralded will occur, hidden beneath the "shadow" of the Most High, "covered" in mystery. If we could imagine these angelic words addressed to us, if we could listen as though this announcement were completely new, we too would be filled with fear and wonder. Think how many *more* questions Mary must have had after this "explanation"!

God responds to our wonder with more wonder.

Even with our greater knowledge of the things that would take place in the months and years after this young girl's encounter with an angel, perhaps Mary understood *more* than we do. As Mary prayed the psalms, the following words must have often passed her lips: "Let me abide in your tent forever, find refuge under the shelter of your wings" (Psalm 61:4). Mary's desire to dwell in the house of the Lord, to find shelter under the wings of the Most High, to live in the splendor of never-ending wonder has been answered.

But what an answer! The world has been turned upside down! The power of the Most High desires to dwell in *her* house, to find shelter under *Mary's* wings!

Through the unprecedented experience of this young girl, the whole of humanity may be, like Mary, *with* God, tucked under those wings of hammered gold. And by the same token, in our littleness, our simplicity, our obscurity, our quiet, and our wonder, God will discover an entry and abide in us.

Prayer

My soul is satisfied as with a rich feast,
　and my mouth praises you with joyful lips
when I think of you on my bed,
　and meditate on you in the watches of the night;
for you have been my help,
　and in the shadow of your wings I sing for joy.

Psalm 63:5–7

oving God,
　　Only open
　　your wings
　　and I will climb beneath their shadow
　　and find holy peace.
　　Amen.

Reading

. . . .And now, your relative Elizabeth in her old age has also conceived a son; and this is the sixth month for her who was said to be barren. For nothing will be impossible with God."

Luke 1:36–37

Reflection

Rifts, divisions, arguments? We *will* be reconciled in loving communion.

Hunger, poverty, loneliness? We *will* be filled to overflowing.

Illness, death, ignorance, sin? We *will* be made splendidly whole.

Exile, wandering, homelessness? We *will* dwell in the everlasting house of the Lord.

"For nothing will be impossible with God."

Can we accept the implication of these words? Seeking an advantage, distancing ourselves from troubling situations, feeling superior or inferior, allowing disappointments and frustrations to harden our hearts, indulging our impatience—if we were truly to *know*, with our whole selves, that nothing at all will be impossible with God, these activities would appear to be a silly waste of time.

When that day comes, how will we fill our hours?

Prayer

Who is like the LORD our God,
   who is seated on high,
who looks far down
   on the heavens and the earth?
He raises the poor from the dust,
   and lifts the needy from the ash heap,
to make them sit with princes,
   with the princes of his people.
He gives the barren woman a home,
   making her the joyous mother of children.
Praise the LORD!

Psalm 113:5–9

I thank you, O Lord, for giving the world
children.
Children are the crown of your method;
through them, you make all things new.
Each child contains
a new heaven and a new earth.
Little ones are the embodiment
of your love.
In the eyes of children, I have glimpsed
the world being born anew, and in their eyes
I, too, am reborn.
Amen.

Reading

Then Mary said, "Here am I, the servant of the Lord; let it be with me according to your word." Then the angel departed from her.

Luke 1:38

Reflection

Thank you, Mary. Thank you with all my heart.

Prayer

Hallelujah!
For the Lord our God
   the Almighty reigns.
Let us rejoice and exult
   and give him the glory,
for the marriage of the Lamb has come,
   and his bride has made herself ready;
to her it has been granted to be clothed
   with fine linen, bright and pure.

Revelation 19:6b–8a

Dear Jesus,
   on the day of my Baptism, I wore a white garment;
   and like Mary before me,
I became your bride.
From that day, my life has been
one continual feast.
As a wedding gift, you gave me
a garment of light, bright and pure.
Because you have chosen me
as your bride, I join your banquet,
singing for joy.
I approach the table you prepare for me
and taste you,
and I remember how you love me,
every moment of your life in my hands
and heart.
You are with me,
You will always be with me,
until the end of time,
according to your word.
Amen.

The Visitation of Mary to Elizabeth

Luke 1:39–45

Reading

In those days Mary set out and went with haste to a Judean town in the hill country.

Luke 1:39

Reflection

The Greek word that Luke uses to describe how Mary set out is so evocative here. *Anastasa* is the word, used in the Septuagint, to translate the Hebrew word *qwm,* which means "to rise." *Anastasa* can thus recall all the moments in Israel's past when someone arose to initiate actions, most particularly actions in accord with the covenant of God, as when God commanded Abram, "Rise up, walk through the length and the breadth of the land, for I will give it to you" (Genesis 13:17). The word also looks forward in anticipation toward the *Anastasa* (the Resurrection) of Christ, who said, "I am the resurrection and the life," and whose blood initiates the new and everlasting covenant we celebrate in the Eucharist.

In what sense did Mary "rise"?

When the angel announced to Mary that the child she was to have would be called "Son of the Most High," she gave her "yes." Then the Holy Spirit came upon her. In that moment, Mary became the first person to consciously follow Christ.

With her "yes" Mary participates in the very life given in Christ, and, filled with the wonder of the Spirit, she is impelled out of her home and into the hill country of Judea.

Once filled with this new life, her first act is to reach out to another person.

Prayer

For I know that my Redeemer lives,
   and that at the last he will stand upon the earth;
and after my skin has been thus destroyed,
   then in my flesh I shall see God.

Job 19:25–26

ou are the Living God;
   you save me from all limits:
   the deaths that steal each moment
and Death that stills the heart.
You redeem all my lost moments
and give them back to me, transformed
to everlasting radiance.
You redeem my wickedness,
making of it a clear lens
through which I can see your glory and peace.
Take all of me,
let me rise up to meet you
in the flesh.
Let me live your abundant life,
even on this earth,
so I may never die.
Amen.

Reading

. . . where she entered the house of Zechariah and greeted Elizabeth.

Luke 1:40

Reflection

How long had Elizabeth been waiting to hear her husband explain why he'd been struck mute? What could she make of her own pregnancy? With Zechariah's silence, Elizabeth does not know what the angel said to her husband in the temple. She does not know how or why this marvelous pregnancy has suddenly overtaken her life. Think of all the theories Elizabeth must have entertained, all her unanswered questions: Who is my husband? Who is this child within me? Who am I?

How did Elizabeth answer herself? Living in this house of silence and questions, she must have been almost bursting with curiosity, waiting and hoping and praying for some sign from God.

It is so uncomfortable not to know the answers, not to be in on the plan. And yet, in our straining toward understanding, answers do come, if we know how to find them. Without this strain, this terrible need we have to make sense of the world, we will not perceive the wonderful when it happens to us.

One day, in this house of thick silence and questions that have no answers, Elizabeth hears a new and completely unexpected voice. In this moment, Elizabeth knows with complete certainty that the answers to all her questions are contained in that one, new voice. How does she know?

Can we imagine the sound of Mary's greeting? Mary must have been tired from her travel and yet terribly eager to see this marvel that the angel had described for her. She must have been worried for her cousin's health, but also overjoyed to see the visible pregnancy, such a blessing for Elizabeth and such a concrete confirmation of all that the angel had foretold. Mary must have also been shy and unsure, wondering how she would tell Elizabeth of her own marvelous pregnancy. She must have worried about whether Elizabeth would believe that Mary's pregnancy was of God. All these complicated emotions would have been present in Mary's voice.

And Elizabeth's ears and her heart had been waiting so long to hear something, anything.

Prayer

Let us come into his presence with thanksgiving;
　let us make a joyful noise to him with songs of praise!
For the LORD is a great God,
　and a great King above all gods.
In his hand are the depths of the earth;
　the heights of the mountains are his also.
The sea is his, for he made it,
　and the dry land, which his hands have formed.

O come, let us worship and bow down,
　let us kneel before the LORD, our Maker!
For he is our God,
　and we are the people of his pasture,
　and the sheep of his hand.

O that today you would listen to his voice!

Psalm 95:2–7

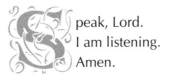

peak, Lord.
I am listening.
Amen.

Reading

When Elizabeth heard Mary's greeting, the child leaped in her womb. And Elizabeth was filled with the Holy Spirit.

Luke 1:41

Reflection

When John leaped in Elizabeth's womb, she knew, in a flash of inspiration: *Mary is here because she too is pregnant! Hers is also an "impossible" pregnancy!* Had she heard these facts in Mary's tone of voice? Did she see them in the way Mary walked, in Mary's pallor, or lack thereof? Could Elizabeth discern, from the way the few simple words were pronounced, the tangled emotions that lived in the young girl's heart?

The Holy Spirit rushes to our aid. In all the small coincidences we notice, in every opportune memory, in what we call "luck," in those chance remarks we blurt before we ask ourselves, *Where in the world did that come from?* These sudden surprise twists bring laughter and tears because they catch us off guard and render us vulnerable to all the wonderful and awful possibilities that we might otherwise overlook: the ironies, the paradoxes, the unexplainable events that suddenly draw our attention and amazement.

Elizabeth's marvelous baby leaps, and she thinks, *Why, Mary must be having a baby, too! An even more marvelous baby! I see joy in Mary's eyes. And my baby's movement felt like pure joy!*

How do we know that these insights come from the Holy Spirit?

Every observation, every look, every word, every gesture that brings about unity is the working of the Holy Spirit. The Holy Spirit is the "glue" that attaches us in love and friendship and compassion to one another; ultimately, it is the Holy Spirit who makes it possible for us to obey Christ's command to remain in his love (John 15). The Holy Spirit reveals the invisible connections among things that at first seem unrelated in order to demonstrate the same connections that bind us, one to another, in Christ.

And then the two women embrace.

Prayer

May all of us who share in the body and blood of Christ
be brought together in unity by the Holy Spirit.

From Eucharistic Prayer II

Come Holy Spirit,
fill me with a desire for reconciliation.
Make the walls come tumbling down!
Dissolve the ideologies
that prevent me from embracing my neighbors.
Give me hope for the glorious impossible,
that I may live your faithful promise
of Parousia,
of universal love.
Amen.

Reading

. . . and exclaimed with a loud cry, "Blessed are you among women, and blessed is the fruit of your womb."

Luke 1:42

Reflection

Elizabeth's skin is still warm from the loving embrace of her young relative. All the complexities, all the mysteries of this meeting between the two women have flooded Elizabeth's heart in an instant. She stands and stares at Mary. What words could possibly measure up to this moment? She doesn't pause to think or to consider whether to make a speech. Elizabeth's heart simply bubbles over with the most pressing thought in her over-awed mind: Blessed!

Praise is the soul of our faith. Mary is blessed, and when we sense this fact, our hearts cry out her praise, not out of duty, not because we want something from her, not in order to impress anyone, but because in the whole history of our lives, nothing and no one so wonderful as Mary has ever greeted us.

And what is the meaning of this word, *blessed?* The Greek word used here is *eulogemēnē,* which refers to the holy praise that is Mary's due. *Eulogemēnē* is the Greek word used in the Septuagint to translate the Hebrew word *barukh,* used in Jewish prayer to extol the Lord.

Together with Elizabeth we exclaim: "Blessed are you among women! And blessed is the fruit of your womb, Jesus!"

Here is the answer to all the questions Elizabeth has harbored during her solitary vigil. Praise will yield the answer to our most pressing needs: for knowledge, insight and wisdom, strength, counsel, wonder and awe, as well as for the burning love that will ignite our hearts during our darkest journeys into the final, most miraculous dawn.

Prayer

Hail, holy Queen, mother of mercy,
our life, our sweetness, and our hope.

From the *Salve Regina*

Blessed Mary,
Grant me the eyes of Elizabeth,
your kinswoman,
that I may truly see you
and experience your blessedness all my days.
Help me to hear your beloved greeting,
that when I hail you, Queen of my heart,
your sweetness and your hope may truly be mine.
Amen.

Reading

And why has this happened to me, that the mother of my Lord comes to me?

Luke 1:43

Reflection

Does Elizabeth's question seem strange? Do we usually ask, "Why?" when we are confronted with something marvelous beyond compare?

Or do we only turn our eyes to heaven, looking for reasons, when calamity hits: "Why me, Lord? What did I do to deserve this?"

We might also ask God why we exist or what purpose our lives should have. These questions remind us that we are alive, that we depend on God. If we pay attention to God's voice in our lives, we find that answers to these questions lead to more questions, that the period of questioning never ends. The life of God's faithful servants is not stable. It is a life driven, not by a purpose formulated by human terms, but by questions. Our only purpose is to listen to the One whose glorious purpose is a mysterious plan for cosmic unity fulfilled in Jesus Christ.

God answers us, but his answers are never pat or even readily intelligible. Think of Saint Francis. God told him to repair his church. As Francis carried stones and laid them in place, one on top of the other, did he know how many brothers and sisters would join him in this work? Did he know that he had begun to repair God's Church? How could he have known that the simple work of carrying stones would result in something so marvelous? His first questions must have been so rudimentary and practical: What sort of stones shall I choose? How do I fashion a doorway? These questions led him, by a path only God could have laid out for him, to newer, more momentous questions: What rule shall I fashion for myself and my brothers? How can I be a means to God for my friends?

Meanwhile, Elizabeth asks an even more wonderful question: "Why has this happened to me that the Mother of my Lord comes to me?"

We don't always seem to be as puzzled by our blessings. When we approach to receive the Eucharist, do we say in our hearts, "Why does this happen to me that my Lord is offering himself to me?" And when we have received the living Christ, Body and Blood, do we ask, "Why does this happen to me that my Lord comes to reside within me?" And then, among our brothers and sisters in Christ, do we ever ask ourselves, "Why does this happen to me that Christ should be present to me in this community?" Do we ever ask, "Why does this happen to me that God has promised he will be all in all things?" The answers to these questions will answer all the others.

"I have said these things to you so that my joy may be in you, and that your joy may be complete" (John 15:11).

Prayer

Rejoice in the Lord always; again I will say, Rejoice. Let your gentleness be known to everyone. The Lord is near. Do not worry about anything, but in everything by prayer and supplication with thanksgiving let your requests be made known to God. And the peace of God, which surpasses all understanding, will guard your hearts and your minds in Christ Jesus.

Philippians 4:4–7

Dear Lord,
Let me always rejoice in you.
Let me be amazed by joy,
and help me always to remember
to ask, again and again,
why this joy should be mine.
Amen.

Reading

For as soon as I heard the sound of your greeting, the child in my womb leaped for joy.

Luke 1:44

Reflection

Scholars sometimes compare Saint John the Baptist's leap in his mother's womb to the violent movement of the twins, Esau and Jacob, in Rebekah's womb: "The children struggled together within Rebekah; and she said, 'If it is to be this way, why do I live?' So she went to inquire of the Lord" (Genesis 25:22). In the Greek Old Testament, the verb used to describe the "struggle" of the twins within Rebekah is the same word used to describe the infant John's "leap" within Elizabeth. But these two stories are more different than they are alike!

The Lord explains to Rebekah that the children within her are struggling because

Two nations are in your womb,
And two peoples born of you shall be divided;
The one shall be stronger than the other,
The elder shall serve the younger.
—Genesis 25:23

But between John and Jesus there will be no struggle, no division. Though John, the elder, will serve Jesus, he does not represent a separate nation. His destiny is intimately connected to the Lord's. Unlike Esau, who sells his birthright for a bowl of stew, John does not swerve from his mission to "go before the Lord to prepare his ways"; instead, even when he is confronted with imprisonment and execution, he clings to the inheritance that God gives him, to be "the prophet of the Most High."

Also, the differences between the two mothers are striking. Rebekah does not understand what is happening in her body and must ask the Lord. She also experiences this movement as pain and complains, "Why do I live?" In contrast, Elizabeth knows why her child leaps. She experiences this movement as joy and also asks, "Why?" but in wonder and astonishment, not in complaint.

In light of these differences, the repetition of the Greek word that Rebekah and Elizabeth share becomes more significant, not less. What is the real difference between these two events? When Rebekah felt the painful sensation in her womb, Mary was not standing before her, bearing Good News beyond compare. What a difference the Incarnation makes! Even in the womb of Mary, Jesus makes all things astonishingly, joyfully *new*.

Prayer

Do not remember the former things,
  or consider the things of old.
I am about to do a new thing;
  now it springs forth, do you not perceive it?
I will make a way in the wilderness
  and rivers in the desert.
The wild animals will honor me,
  the jackals and the ostriches;
for I give water in the wilderness,
  rivers in the desert,
to give drink to my chosen people,
  the people whom I formed for myself
so that they might declare my praise.

Isaiah 43:18–21

pring of Living Water,
    gush from my heart.
    Let my thirst for you
  be my drink.
  Let me see that everything you do
  is always, and always will be,
  forever new.
  Amen.

Reading

And blessed is she who believed that there would be
a fulfillment of what was spoken to her by the Lord.

Luke 1:45

Reflection

Here we find the first beatitude in the Gospel of Luke. This word,
blessed, is actually a different word from the one Elizabeth spoke
before, when she said, "Blessed are you among women and blessed is
the fruit of your womb, Jesus." Instead of using *eulogemēnē,* Elizabeth
now says, *makaria,* which has a different shade of meaning.

The first time Elizabeth blesses Mary, she means to exclaim that
Mary is "most praise-worthy" and "to be extolled" by God, from
whom all blessings flow. But now, with the word *makaria,* Elizabeth
wishes to express something about Mary's interior life. This new
"blessedness" describes Mary's condition of inner joy.

When Mary exclaims, "Surely, from now on, all generations will
call me blessed, . . ." she means to say that all will recognize and
proclaim her joy. It is barely possible for any of us to imagine such
joy, except that we, too, are invited to bear Christ to the world.
Because Mary is blessed, then, we may be called blessed as well.
"The Mighty One does great things for us! And holy is his name!"

Later, when Jesus proclaims that the poor, the hungry, and the
persecuted are blessed, he also uses the word *makaria* to express that
these people are full of joy. Their joy springs from the same source
as Mary's joy. They realize, along with Mary, that the kingdom is
at hand. For when Elizabeth says, "that there would be a fulfillment
of what was spoken to her by the Lord," she is speaking of the Lord's
promise of salvation for the end of time, of Parousia, when God
will be "all in all." Those who have eyes to see this glorious reality
are known by their joy, no matter what their present, earthly
circumstances.

Prayer

For I am about to create new heavens
    and a new earth;
the former things shall not be remembered
    or come to mind.
But be glad and rejoice forever
    in what I am creating;
for I am about to create Jerusalem as a joy,
    and its people as a delight.
I will rejoice in Jerusalem,
    and delight in my people.

        Isaiah 65:17–19a

 y God, you are always
    about to create
    in joy and delight.
Because I must live in time,
each present moment exists
stretched between a past moment
and a future joy.
Absolute fulfillment
is eternity transformed into now.
But eternity is not static or dead.
It lives! It grows!
Open my eyes that I may see eternal life,
your joy unfolding in timeless wonder.
Amen.

The Parable of the Ten Bridesmaids

❧

Matthew 25:1–12

Reading

Then the kingdom of heaven will be like this. Ten bridesmaids took their lamps and went to meet the bridegroom.

Matthew 25:1

Reflection

Jesus tells us that the kingdom of heaven is movement. We are all on a journey. We are going to meet the bridegroom.

But wait. Isn't Christ already here? Isn't he speaking to us now, at this very moment, in these words about a wedding feast? These bridesmaids, who have somewhere *to go,* can't have anything to do with us. Then, perhaps we are the bride, not mentioned here, yet essential to any wedding.

When God initiated the covenant with Abraham and his descendants, he espoused himself to a people. Israel became his bride: "For your Maker is your husband, the LORD of hosts is his name" (Isaiah 54:5a). And those who attend to God's chosen people are themselves among the chosen. They are both bridesmaids and bride.

Could we simply consider ourselves the bride and disregard the fate of bridesmaids, foolish or wise? Or are we called, in some way, to serve God's bride, his chosen people?

In the same chapter of Matthew, Jesus says,

> Then the king will say to those at his right hand, "Come, you that are blessed by my Father, inherit the kingdom prepared for you from the foundation of the world, for I was hungry and you gave me food, I was thirsty and you gave me something to drink, I was a stranger and you welcomed me, I was naked and you gave me clothing, I was sick and you took care of me, I was in prison and you visited me." Matthew 25:34–40

Here we have an explicit description of the duties of a bridesmaid. All but the most wretched, weakest members of God's chosen people may fulfill these duties.

Then perhaps the oil represents good works? No. Any of these works may be performed out of fear, sterile duty, or desire for a reward.

Only work done out of great love will qualify us to be wise bridesmaids.

Each moment of freely given love is complete, like a perfect pearl. But out of respect for our freedom, love demands that in each new moment of our lives we choose again, whether to embrace love, in all its newness, and thus form a new pearl. In this way, the lives of saints become as a string of matchless pearls, hanging from the golden thread of God's grace. Even saints cannot escape living the tension between the ecstasy of the present and the anticipation of their next step into uncertainty, when Christ will ask again, "Do you love me?"

Yes, Christ is already here. Aware of the dignity and honor of our position, we sit at his feet, safe in the halo of eternity that is his holy unquenchable light. And now, we do listen with our whole selves; however, we cannot escape the awareness that in an instant, as we confront the next moment, we will have to turn again to the light. Then we will have to decide, in total freedom, whether we will remain with him and whether we will feed his sheep.

Prayer

But he placed his right hand on me, saying, "Do not be afraid; I am the first and the last, and the living one. I was dead, and see, I am alive forever and ever.

Revelation 1:17b–18a

Living King
of a living kingdom, please
wake me to the fullness of your life
that is so much more intense and alive
than anything I have yet experienced!
Let me please participate in your
divine vitality
and let me share it with all I meet.
Amen.

Reading

Five of them were foolish, and five were wise.

Matthew 25:2

Reflection

How beautiful that we *want* to be wise; we *want* to be among
the chosen.

But will God make us wise if we ask him? Let's not imagine that
the answer to this question is easy. We have known people who, in
the sincerity of their hearts, have asked for wisdom, but they don't
seem so very wise to us.

In fact, many people invoke wisdom, but few receive it.

Many want wisdom to adorn them, like a precious ornament.
Others use the word *wisdom* to stamp their approval upon the ideas
they think are worthy. Others confuse wisdom with knowledge
concerning doctrine, with intelligence, with the gift of good inter-
pretation, or even with a reliable memory!

Wisdom is God's method. When we participate in God's plan,
we become the instruments of wisdom. We do not use wisdom,
wisdom uses us. In order to be wise, we surrender our knowledge,
surrender our intelligence, surrender our ability to interpret and
penetrate meaning, even surrender our memories to God. We place
them at the foot of the manger. If we clutch them too tightly, or use
them to illuminate ourselves, or bestow them on objects and people
unworthy of our gifts, we are foolish indeed! Waste is offering
ourselves in the service of nothingness, of darkness.

Wisdom is the power unleashed when we place our gifts in the
service of God.

Prayer

You desire truth in the inward being;
therefore teach me wisdom in my secret heart.

Psalm 51:6

Jesus, you are the way, the truth,
and the life.
If you will abide in my inward being,
then I will have no need
to ask for wisdom!
Amen.

Reading

When the foolish took their lamps, they took no oil with them;
but the wise took flasks of oil with their lamps.

Matthew 25:3–4

Reflection

Oil is a very suggestive substance. It can heal and soothe and clean.
As in this parable, it can burn, with a clean flame. Oil, like the kingdom of God, can spread. Its perfume diffuses into the air, gladdening
all who breathe its scent. Oil shares all these properties with the
action of the Holy Spirit. The Spirit heals and soothes and purifies;
it keeps the light of Christ burning in us and is the means through
which God has communicated his plan of salvation to prophets and
evangelists. The Holy Spirit gladdens an ever-widening circle of
believers, beginning with Mary, who becomes pregnant with God,
in the person of Jesus, God's anointed. In the sacraments of the Church,
the Holy Spirit, when we ask for his grace, transforms our simple gifts
of bread and wine, transforms our relationships, transforms us.

The oil of gladness, needed to illuminate the great wedding banquet
of the bridegroom, is a substance, like olive oil, pressed from the
kernel of a fruit. But what is this fruit?

Jesus said, "I am the vine, you are the branches. Those who abide
in me and I in them bear much fruit, because apart from me you can
do nothing" (John 15:5). This marvelous fruit from Jesus grows when
we *love one another* as he has loved us. This fruit is a result of love,
the divine love that flows from Christ to us and among his beloved.
Without an expansive, self-giving, inclusive, and infinitely forgiving
Christ-like love, a branch can bear no fruit, can do nothing.

In order to produce oil, a fruit must first be broken and consumed,
the inner seed crushed, and a tiny quantity of precious liquid extracted
from its meat. The process of making wine or bread also requires
that the original fruit be crushed and its essential qualities discovered
and harvested. Christ himself underwent this process when he was
incarnated as an infant and then again when he was crucified.

When we were anointed, at Baptism and again in Confirmation, (and yet again if we've received the Anointing of the Sick), we participated in the qualities of the holy oil we received. In accepting this precious gift and embracing it with joy, we ourselves became oil, a balm for this world of pain, a fuel to burn with God's truth, a sweet perfume to gladden all who know us. That small, essential kernel at the center of our being was cracked open, and we became one with Christ, broken and restored, hidden in the tomb and then revealed, crushed to death and resurrected to new life.

Is it a surprise that Jesus loved to pray near the oil press, in the Garden of Gethsemane? The events of his Passion were initiated there, among the olive trees. A seed may die in the earth and produce great fruit. It may also die in a press and yield the oil of gladness.

Prayer

After your Son, Jesus Christ our Lord,
asked John for baptism in the waters of Jordan,
you sent the Spirit upon him
in the form of a dóve
and by the witness of your own voice
you declared him to be your only, well-beloved Son.
In this you clearly fulfilled the prophecy of David,
that Christ would be anointed with the oil of gladness
beyond his fellow men.

From the Rite of Consecration of the Chrism, 25

ord of Israel,
Savior, King, and holy Anointed One of God,
press me, crush me, purify me
so I might experience the joy of your Resurrection,
and find my true purpose—
as balm for the world.
Amen.

Reading

As the bridegroom was delayed, all of them became drowsy and slept. But at midnight there was a shout, "Look! Here is the bridegroom! Come out to meet him." Then all those bridesmaids got up and trimmed their lamps. The foolish said to the wise, "Give us some of your oil, for our lamps are going out." But the wise replied, "No! There will not be enough for you and for us; you had better go to the dealers and buy some for yourselves."

Matthew 25:5–9

Reflection

The "foolish" bridesmaids are not called "evil." And yet they dwell outside, in the "evil" dark, because they did not buy enough oil. From other parables Jesus told, we understand that "buying" is a vitally important activity if we wish to enter into the kingdom of heaven. The merchant sells all he owns to buy one precious pearl. A man buys a field after he discovers that it contains a hidden treasure.

These bridesmaids are not ignorant of the wedding; being brides-maids, they have been introduced to the wedding party, so just as the merchant and the man who finds treasure, the bridesmaids have "found" the kingdom. Finding is not enough. Selling all one has is not enough. We need to "buy" the divine life, to embrace the kingdom of God. Not to "buy" the key element, when we are faced with it, means not to commit one's whole heart to God.

When the foolish ask for oil, the wise refuse and send them off to the "dealers," because no one can share an inner commitment with someone else, and this essential pledge cannot be divided into portions.

What is the price of "enough" oil? All that we are, all that we have. Each of us must love God with *all* our hearts, *all* our souls, *all* our strength, and *all* our minds.

Prayer

Bless the LORD, O my soul,
  and all that is within me,
  bless his holy name.

Psalm 103:1

Dearest Jesus,
I give you all that I am
or ever will be. I give you
all the secret parts of me
that I do not even comprehend.
I wish to offer myself,
exactly as I am,
to you.
Amen.

Reading

And while they went to buy it, the bridegroom came, and those who were ready went with him into the wedding banquet; and the door was shut. Later the other bridesmaids came also, saying, "Lord, lord, open to us." But he replied, "Truly I tell you, I do not know you."

Matthew 25:10–12

Reflection

In some sense, we are all too late. We all remember events we were not prepared for, times when we failed to pledge our whole selves to God. There are so many missed opportunities, occasions when we might have entered into the fullness of Christ's love, but instead we chose the lesser, poorer path. Even when we receive absolution for these times, they are not blotted from our memories. We may still suffer sharp regret from past actions.

But let's make certain right now, with all that we have, that Christ knows us. Let's open ourselves, in all our frailty and complexity and beauty, to him. We can turn our faces to him and say, "Here I am, Lord." Then no matter how many doors remain closed behind us, the one in front of us will open wide.

We are going to meet the bridegroom!

Prayer

Listen! I am standing at the door, knocking; if you hear my voice and open the door, I will come in to you and eat with you, and you with me.

Revelation 3:20

ord Jesus Christ,
I welcome you into my whole self.
I have been preparing this banquet
my whole life.
Only say the word,
and I shall be made worthy
to serve you.
Amen.

Micah's Prophecy
of Bethlehem

❧

Micah 5:2a

Reading

But you, O Bethlehem of Ephrathah . . .

Micah 5:2a

Reflection

Bethlehem (when Jesus was born there) is a place so distant from our lives, so unfamiliar to us. Do we dare try to imagine its streets, its buildings, its open areas? What food did they cook over their simple fires? They must have eaten olives, grapes, and bread. What was the texture of the cloth worn by its people? When the sun beat down by day, was it brighter and hotter than it is for us, here, today? Did it trace a different path in the sky? Night in Bethlehem was certainly deeper in the absence of electric light. Multitudinous stars, like spilled sugar, would have paved the sky; yet we cannot imagine their exact positions or the most particular luminosity of each heavenly body as it appeared on that holy night, two thousand years ago.

If we were to spend our entire lives studying the history and customs of this little town, still we could never recreate how it actually was on that miraculous night when a new star appeared. And if we were to visit Bethlehem today, we would see it through the eyes of a stranger.

How can we then approach Bethlehem? Can we, too, pay homage to our infant king?

As the words of the prophet are living words, spoken by God, Bethlehem lives, and will live through eternity. Because the prophet is also addressing us when he says, "But you, . . ." that eternal Bethlehem dwells within us. For this reason, if we will but look up into the night sky of our own very particular lives, we will surely see, this very evening, a new star.

Prayer

May the Morning Star which never sets find this flame still burning;
Christ, that Morning Star, who came back from the dead, and shed
his peaceful light on all mankind. . .

From the *Exsultet,* the Easter Proclamation

ear Morning Star!
Even now your radiance
brings peace to my soul.
This peace is my own Bethlehem,
where all time belongs to you,
where your quiet, hidden birth
continues to astonish
my heart.
One day,
you will be born anew
to this world, groaning in labor pangs
to receive you
in utter radiance!
Amen.

Reading

. . . who are one of the little clans of Judah,
from you shall come forth for me
   one who is to rule in Israel.

Micah 5:2b

Reflection

Once we see and recognize the star of Bethlehem, our next task will be to follow it to the stable, within which the Lord of the entire cosmos lies enthroned in a manger.

When we stand before a small, defenseless child, we are given an unspoken choice. We are capable of using the vulnerable to further our own ends, or we may choose to step back and allow that which is weaker to exist as it is, to grow and even to thrive.

There are ways to exploit another without resorting to King Herod's methods! We can impose our opinions, our ideologies and personal theories about God onto those who are weaker than we are. We can oppress them with definitions that limit their horizons and then impose diagnoses when they do not accept our approach. We can bribe or frighten them into acknowledging our greatness. We can project our desires and needs onto them, we can publish papers about them without ever consulting them. We can blame them for our failure to reach them and for the unhappiness we inflict upon them.

If we are truthful with ourselves, we will recognize that all knowledge, all truth, all that is, was, and ever shall be comes from God. We do not reach ourselves, "come to ourselves" (as the son in the parable of the forgiving father) without first facing the reality of God, a reality so much larger than we could possibly grasp.

Before God, each of us embodies the littleness of Bethlehem.

God has prepared the entire cosmos for our delight. Within this sacred universe, God, out of reverence for our littleness, invites us to exercise our freedom. We may also call this holy space, given by God, "Bethlehem." We inhabit this place, so huge for us and so tiny for God, in awe and gratitude. Within our Bethlehem, we approach the stable, our Church, where we find a new manger, the altar, where Christ manifests in a bit of crushed, baked wheat.

How little is the morsel of bread we cradle in our hands!

And how little we are before the mystery contained in that morsel!

Let us bow our heads before every gift that God places in our hands. Let us see the weak, the vulnerable, and the children in the bread that we adore, and may we give the gift of Bethlehem.

Prayer

I have calmed and quieted my soul,
  like a weaned child with its mother;

Psalm 131:2a

ear Christ child,
    that you agreed to sleep, helpless,
    on a bed of straw,
  in a stable, in tiny Bethlehem
  for me! For me!
  Only love
  could embrace such weakness,
  my love.
  Please make of me
  a stable, all fresh hay and warm breath of animals.
  I would like to be snug,
  quiet, still.
  Make my roof water-tight
  and my floor clean and level
  for you, my soul. For you!
  Amen.

Isaiah's Prophecy of the Naming of the Messiah

❧

Isaiah 9:6

Reading

For a child has been born for us,
    a son given to us;
authority rests upon his shoulders . . .

Isaiah 9:6a

Reflection

The child is *for us*. The son is *given* to us.

So often religious practice has involved people making offerings to God. We imagine that we can take action on behalf of God, for God. We desire to please God, to assuage God, maybe even to influence God so that he will help us with whatever projects we may be engaged in. If we go to daily Mass *for* God, perhaps God will cure our sickness. If we say a novena *for* the souls in purgatory, perhaps God will help us pass a test. If we live virtuous lives *for* Jesus, perhaps God will reward us, if only with a feeling of satisfaction. How many prayers have been offered in order to bend the will of God to our will!

We waste our breath. God is *for* us, his child given *to* us, but we can do nothing *for* God or *to* God.

God takes the initiative. God is the one who gives. Our giving is, at best, a participation in the larger movement of giving, which is God's action in the world. We cannot give anything to God, because *everything* we have is already a gift: the air we breathe, the hands with which we work, our hearts, the impulse to generosity. Even our sense of gratitude is a gift to us, perhaps one of the greatest gifts we can receive, because the essence of gratitude is grace.

It is a sin to waste any of God's gifts, including the gift of our breath! Let us pray, *Your will be done,* in joyful amazement, recalling that God's will is to give us so much more than we can ask for. We can pray to receive truly, with hearts open, what has already been given: *May this wonderful child be born for us now, here.* We can pray that the gifts this child bears to a lost and wandering humanity might bring us all home to God's dwelling place.

God is *for* us, given *to* us, and he is *with* us too, as Emmanuel. When we begin to sense the truth about God's astonishing generosity, we are deeply grateful to remain in his presence and serve. Only *through* him, *with* him, and *in* him may we offer him the one thing he desires from us: our entire selves, offered spontaneously, in total freedom. No strings attached, no bargains, no commercial transactions. God, with supernatural patience, waits for a response to his unmatched generosity. May we receive the grace to see his goodness, and may we, full of adoration and praise, let go of our human wishes enough to love him with our whole hearts.

Prayer

If God is for us, who is against us? He who did not withhold his own Son, but gave him up for all of us, will he not with him also give us everything else?

Romans 8:31b–32

earest God,
I promise
to spend my life always looking
for your gifts, seeking the Good News
in hidden and open places,
so that my life will be
constant appreciation
and unending delight,
in the All that you give.
Amen.

Reading

. . . and he is named
Wonderful Counselor . . .

Isaiah 9:6b

Reflection

A counselor gives advice. What sort of advice do we receive from Jesus? We must love our enemies. We must pray in secret. We must store up treasure in heaven. Yes, these sayings of Jesus provide us with "advice." When we try to follow this advice, we begin to see just how "wonderful" these teachings are—wonderfully difficult, if not impossible! Perhaps we can convince ourselves that we love our enemies, but would God, who sees into the marrow of our souls, recognize this provisional, anemic, "theoretical" sentiment as love? When we pray, do we ever reach into those secret places in the heart, the corners we reserve for our own plans and intrigues? Do we treasure God, in all his mystery and magnanimity, or do we prefer some by-product of the religious life that brings us comfort, the respect of those we wish to impress, a sense of belonging, or easy righteousness?

Another definition of the word *counselor* is one who plans, who has a deliberate purpose or design. If we examine this meaning more closely, we understand, with true wonder, that this child who is given to us is of God. From the beginning, out of the divine compassion that is his nature, God has had a plan to bring all the created world into the unity and glory of his eternal joy. The centerpiece of God's counsel, his loving design, has been to make creatures in his own image, filled with his breath and aided by the Holy Spirit, who would freely cooperate with this plan for fulfillment. When the time came, he gave us himself, in the person of Jesus Christ, in order to allure us.

God's method is allurement.

The "advice" that Jesus gives is never meant to discourage; rather, his counsel invites us to a gorgeous banquet. In loving our enemies, we see the face of Christ, who loves all. When we pray, we illuminate our whole selves and merge with the light that prevails. Throwing away all earthly gain frees us to live in constant wonder. These are some means we have been given so that we might live the life of Christ, the counselor of a wonderful and total peace that surpasses all understanding.

Prayer

With all wisdom and insight he has made known to us the mystery of his will, according to his good pleasure that he set forth in Christ, as a plan for the fullness of time, to gather up all things in him, things in heaven, and things on earth.

Ephesians 1:8b–10

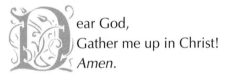

ear God,
Gather me up in Christ!
Amen.

Reading

... Mighty God ...

Isaiah 9:6b

Reflection

Here we discover the paradox at the heart of God's self revelation.
Our mighty God comes to us as a helpless child. What happens
when we place these two images side by side? Do the two pictures
seem to cancel one another?

Once I saw an elderly, distinguished man peer into the face of
a newborn baby girl. Eyes filled with delight, he exclaimed, "She
slays me!"

God, our Mighty Father, has the power to slay us, but he only
exercises his power in this narrow sense. Before false accusations, the
power of empire, the bite of nail and slash of spear, he will slay us by
accepting his own death.

Will we succumb to his might? Will we bend over the manger,
along with Mary and Joseph, peer into his face, and exclaim in our
hearts, "He slays me!"?

Prayer

But I will sing of your might;
 I will sing aloud of your steadfast love in the morning.
For you have been a fortress for me
 and a refuge in the day of my distress.
O my strength, I will sing praises to you,
 for you, O God, are my fortress,
 the God who shows me steadfast love.

Psalm 59:16–17

ear Jesus,
 How hard it is to accept your might
 and to pattern my life upon it.
 Can such vulnerability really be my fortress?
 Only through your strengthening love
 can I even contemplate
 making myself weak and helpless.
 But I will do it, Lord. I will give up
 all my defenses
 and live in your love.
 Amen.

Reading

... Everlasting Father ...

Isaiah 9:6b

Reflection

God, through his ever-living Word, is the master weaver of a glorious tapestry whose name is *eternity*. Eternity is the expression of God's delight, the substance of divine life, and the texture of God's everlasting covenant with humankind.

We are the threads. We may choose to stay as single threads, fragile and delimited. Then in time we will fray and snap. Or we can place ourselves into the hands of God, who will weave us into the strong fabric of his own eternal joy.

Prayer

He has set in order the splendors of his wisdom;
   he is from all eternity one and the same.
Nothing can be added or taken away,
   and he needs no one to be his counselor.

Sirach 42:21

ather of all the living,
   You placed an infinite hunger
   in my heart. Let me never settle
for anything less
than your eternity.
Amen.

❧

Reading

. . . Prince of Peace. . . .

Isaiah 9:6b

Reflection

The child is heir to a kingdom called "Peace." Can we visit this kingdom? Can we live there? Will someone bring a globe and point to this place?

When once the door of our own longing has been flung open, we become pilgrims on a journey. Like Abraham, we step off the known world into a desert where all directions look the same. Even though we do not know where we are headed, and though we have no map, we feel ourselves inexorably drawn forward by a voice that calls us by name. The greatest amazement is that, if we listen, at each point along the way we will have already arrived at our destination.

Some of Abraham's associates and neighbors believed that God was in a particular rock. Others worshipped God on a particular mountain. As they traveled away from that rock or that mountain, they thought that they would move further and further from God. But God wanted Abraham to know that he was the God of all places and times. Abraham could worship God no matter where God led him, and his conversation with God could continue, uninterrupted, no matter the location, under any circumstances. God unifies the diversity of existence through his constant presence and activity in every element of the cosmos.

The desert still surrounds us. We cannot see any path except the one we ourselves prepare, with only our own two hands to do the work. Behind us, the way we have traveled is swallowed in shifting sands. But where we stand right now is the very spot where God initiated the ongoing conversation with Abraham. To listen to God is our birthright. To respond is to inherit a rich land, a promised land flowing with milk and honey, a land called "Unity," where the only law is everlasting peace.

Bring me a globe and I will point to the kingdom of Peace, where the child will reign as Prince. Now look closely. Do you see? He is here.

Prayer

For the mountains may depart
   and the hills be removed,
but my steadfast love shall not depart from you,
   and my covenant of peace shall not be removed,
says the LORD, who has compassion on you.

   Isaiah 54:10

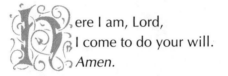ere I am, Lord,
I come to do your will.
Amen.

The Season
of Christmas

The Magnificat:
A Prayer for
Christmas Eve

❧

Taken from Luke 1:46–56

And Mary said,
"My soul magnifies the Lord,
    and my spirit rejoices in God my Savior,
for he has looked with favor on the lowliness of his servant.
    Surely, from now on all generations will call me blessed;
for the Mighty One has done great things for me,
    and holy is his name."

Luke 1:46–49

ord God of all creation, allow my soul to become
a lens to gather and focus and concentrate your light
to a point.
Allow me to add my speck of praise to the Grandeur that is,
was, and ever shall be.
Allow someone, in beholding me,
to comprehend a wider view of your infinity.
Make me transparent, that anyone could see,
through me,
the Love that moves the cosmos.

His mercy is for those who fear him
From generation to generation.

Luke 1:50

our mercy is always there, always
available, always outlasting
the interval between my first breath and my last.
I know that your mercy will enfold my children,
and my children's children
with a strength and finality I can never possess.
And so I offer myself up entirely to your mercy;
please let it carry my prayer for peace
into every generation.

He has shown strength with his arm;
he has scattered the proud in the thoughts of their hearts.

Luke 1:51

lease erase my proud thoughts
and remove me from my bubble of superiority.
Instead, make me small and quiet and attentive
and alive to your work
so that I may seek unity
in all I see and hear,
in every syllable I utter,
in all the thoughts of my heart.
Gather me up in your embrace.

He has brought down the powerful from their thrones,
and lifted up the lowly;

Luke 1:52

od, your Son stooped
to wash the feet of his followers.
Grant that I may stoop
and stoop again,
and never once wish for any throne
except for the one I make
with my own cupped hands
when I approach
your altar.

He has filled the hungry with good things,
and sent the rich away empty.

Luke 1:53

am so rich:
rich in talents, rich in gifts.
But so often life sends me away empty!
Help me to understand
that to you all my talents
are poor compared to my hunger for you.
Let me count my hunger as my richest gift.
Make me always hungry
for the More that is you.

He has helped his servant Israel,
in remembrance of his mercy,
according to the promise he made to our ancestors,
to Abraham and to his descendants forever.

Luke 1:54–55

n your presence is fulfillment
of every promise, even the ones
that I never had the ears to hear.
Today is the day you have made.
I rejoice! I celebrate with all my heart!
I believe.
Amen.

O, Come Let Us Adore: A Reflection and Prayer for Christmas Day

ॐ

Based on Luke 2:7

And she gave birth to her firstborn son . . . .

Luke 2:7a

God, who caused the stars to explode into light merely by speaking a word, who initiated and guided the evolution of all matter, until our earth brought forth this miraculous abundance of life, the same God who has formed us out of primordial stardust, saw that we were filled with wonder, awestruck by all he had done.

Yet God wanted more for us.

And so God entered this history, which he himself had created. He freely accepted the laws of gravity and decay that govern our temporal lives, so that he could become a human being, one of us. Why? Why would God do any such thing?

Jesus has told us that he is the Good Shepherd, that he calls us each *by name*. By this, Jesus means to say that he knows each of us on a cellular level, that his knowledge of us penetrates to the core of all our thoughts and desires. God knows us, and he wants us to know him, too. He sent Jesus so that we could meet with him, listen to his words, abide in him, fall in love with him. Without knowledge, we cannot love anything or anyone.

So, we ask ourselves, "Who is Jesus? Who are you, Lord?"

We sometimes grow complacent, thinking we already know the answer and that God has no more to teach us (!), until some word from scripture, some moment in Mass when we are particularly attentive, suddenly opens up a new awareness, a new set of questions. Like any beloved person, Christ is ultimately mysterious. Unlike other people, he embodies mystery, the ultimate Mystery, the mystery of our very existence.

At Christmas we celebrate the awesome Gift that God began to answer our questions about himself and our life in him, using the most explicable language we have, the substance of our very lives. We now know that God is a baby, born into poverty in an occupied land. What does God mean for us to know about him, given these facts? How does this event, which occurred in Bethlehem over two thousand years ago, help us to answer our questions?

Who is Jesus? Who are you, Lord?

Parents and all those who have loved children have been given a particular blessing. We know babies. We have awaited their births, we have held them and cared for them. What has this knowledge taught us about our infant God?

Love must be the moving force in the universe.

O, come let us adore him.

Prayer

I led them with cords of human kindness,
  with bands of love.
I was to them like those
  who lift infants to their cheeks.
  I bent down to them and fed them.

Hosea 11:4

You came to me as an infant so that I might lift you to my cheek,
  bend down to you,
  and feed you.
Because you give yourself to me,
a precious and vulnerable baby,
I may gaze upon you,
nestled in my very own arms!
Only now can I begin to imagine
the joy of your heart
as you cradle me.
Amen.

The Birth of
Jesus Christ and
the Adoration
of the Shepherds

❧

Luke 2:1–20

Reading

In those days a decree went out from Emperor Augustus that all
the world should be registered. This was the first registration
and was taken while Quirinius was governor of Syria. All went
to their own towns to be registered.

Luke 2:1–3

Reflection

Here was the political reality into which the Christ child would be
born: the earthly government exercised its seemingly limitless power
through a decree that "all the world" must be counted and registered
by name.

But counting and naming are the prerogatives of God alone:
"He determines the number of the stars; he gives to all of them their
names" (Psalm 147:4). Only the Good Shepherd knows all his sheep
by name. Who was the Emperor Augustus to set himself up as a god?
He was so tiny in relation to the child who was born on his watch,
and yet at this moment in history, he appeared to be the one pulling
the strings.

Irony is at work here.

What a sense of control the emperor must have felt. As a result of
his decree, people were dislocated, their lives thrown into disarray.
Could he have had any regard for the tiny, hidden lives that he
disrupted? And yet God, who knows each person so intimately, used
this occasion to fulfill the words of his prophets. For now Joseph was
obliged to travel with his wife to Bethlehem, where Micah
prophesied that the one who is to rule in Israel would be born, a
journey Joseph never would have dreamed of undertaking without
the emperor's decree. And there Mary gave birth to Jesus, of whom
the prophet Isaiah had written, "authority rests on his shoulder."

Only God has the power to control our destiny, and what is amazing
is that he doesn't exercise that power. Out of love God invites, he calls
each of us by name, but he will never force his faithful ones to do
anything. God invites us to write our own destiny.

Augustus' display of power foreshadows the words of Pontius Pilate at Jesus' trial: "Do you not know that I have the power to release you, and the power to crucify you?" This power that Pilate believes he has is akin to Augustus' power to count and to take down people's names. Both are illusory. Jesus answers all earthly princes when he tells Pilate, "You would have no power over me unless it had been given you from above" (John 19:11a).

So, in these two great moments in Jesus' life, Roman lords seem to be controlling events; meanwhile, God's love is the moving force behind all events. His love is the great and mysterious event that breathes life into all that is, the Great Light that shines in the darkness of human history, a light made manifest on earth, during the reign of the Emperor Augustus, in a human child.

Prayer

My frame was not hidden from you,
when I was being made in secret,
    intricately woven in the depths of the earth.
Your eyes beheld my unformed substance.
In your book were written
    all the days that were formed for me,
    when none of them as yet existed.

Psalm 139:15–16

 God, I have been "registered"
in your heart, engraved on the palm of your hand.
You number all the hairs of my head.
My secret thoughts are never hidden from you.
Even before my parents named me, you had called me
by name.
Amen.

Reading

Joseph also went from the town of Nazareth in Galilee to Judea, to the city of David called Bethlehem, because he was descended from the house and family of David.

Luke 2:4

Reflection

The name *David* is repeated twice in this verse, and so often throughout the early passages in Luke's Gospel.

David's name has been kept alive throughout human history because, for God's faithful ones, it means "hope."

God promised Abraham children and land. He kept his promise. God promised to bring those children out of slavery. He kept that promise as well. God took the children of Abraham as his bride and gave them the precious gift of the law, so that they might live together in peace. And then, during a golden moment in the history of these children, God gave them a leader who brought protection and peace and who composed a celestial music that could lead them into the heart of God. King David's reign was yet another promise that God made to the children of Abraham. The prophet Isaiah put that promise into words when he wrote, "A shoot shall come out from the stump of Jesse / and a branch shall grow out of his roots" (Isaiah 11:1).

For those who had pondered the marvelous gifts of God throughout all of history and had discerned his hand in the creation of the world, in the care and protection given to Noah, in the great promise made to Abraham, and in the mighty strength of his arm when he collaborated with Moses to lead the Israelites out of Egypt, King David was yet one more indication of glory still to come. King David embodied a promise, and the prophets and holy ones know that God has kept every promise he has made.

Even in the centuries of great darkness, King David's voice had sung so often in their own throats. His music was ever on their lips. In the words of David's precious psalms, the Promise of all promises took human form, enlivened by divine breath: "The Lord is my shepherd, I shall not want."

Prayer

Remember your word to your servant,
    in which you have made me hope.
This is my comfort in my distress,
    that your promise gives me life.

Psalm 119:49–50

ord,
    I place all my hope
    in your Promise,
        for your Promise is your Word, spoken
        from the beginning of the world.
        This life that I receive from your Promise
        is an *eternal* life:
        therefore, according to your Word,
        I am present at the creation of the world,
        I am delivered from the choking waters of the deep;
        in your Promise, you have brought me out of slavery
        into a land flowing with milk and honey.
        Lord God, *You* are my milk, *you* are my honey.
        Amen.

Reading

He went to be registered with Mary, to whom he was engaged and who was expecting a child.

Luke 2:5

Reflection

There are so many things we don't know about Mary and Joseph. How long was their journey from Nazareth to Bethlehem? What did they speak about along the way? We don't even know if Mary was able to ride on a donkey, as artists through the centuries have assumed, or whether she had to walk the entire way to the city of David. A good novel would include these details, but the Bible drops a veil of silence over them.

Over the centuries, people have wondered about the events the Bible does not describe. They have found bits and snatches of information in other sources. Some have speculated about the elements that aren't included in the Bible. Human sympathy can fill many gaps.

We wish to know these lost details because we love Mary, Joseph, and Jesus. We long to accompany them with every step of their journey. If only we could see through their eyes, hear what their ears heard! Sometimes, not knowing these things feels like being banished, locked into our moment in history, forever cut off from the living reality of the Incarnation.

Love makes us desire this knowledge, but there is another sort of love, a love that averts its gaze and blushes in the presence of the beloved. In fact, the most beautiful and meaningful experiences are always hidden. Much as we love them, Mary and Joseph are not our property. In the face of their human dignity, we take a step back and acknowledge that our own greatest, highest moments of existence don't, and can't, take place on a stage.

Luke never records the moment when Jesus was conceived or the particular details of his human birth. And his passage from death to the risen life is "buried" forever behind a large stone. These are mysterious and holy events upon which we cannot and must not trespass.

And yet, in this life we experience our own personal conceptions, our own private births, our own mysterious conversions, when the Resurrection of Christ takes hold of us and transforms us. Most particularly in the Eucharist, we live the whole history of salvation and enter into the deepest mysteries of Christ's life. In this way, God allows us to draw near to the secrets that lie veiled at the heart of the Gospel. In our own trials and triumphs, as well as in holy Communion, those hidden Bible verses take on flesh and blood. If we approach them with reverence and awe, "reading" them with the eyes of Christ, they begin to breathe.

Prayer

But there are also many other things that Jesus did; if every one of them were written down, I suppose that the world itself could not contain the books that would be written.

John 21:25

    our life, oh Lord, is so rich!
    So many mysterious events, hidden forever
    from my eyes!
And yet you have already written
all the things I will ever do.
Nothing I do or feel is too ordinary
for the loving attention of your heart.
Amen.

Reading

While they were there, the time came for her to deliver her child. And she gave birth to her firstborn son and wrapped him in bands of cloth, and laid him in a manger, because there was no place for them in the inn.

Luke 2:6–7

Reflection

After Jesus ascended into heaven, there were many who believed that his time on earth had ended. Many even believed that Jesus was dead! But, as the author of the Acts of the Apostles, Luke knew very well that Christ had kept his promise to stay with us always, by remaining as a living presence in the lives of his apostles, who are *clothed with power from on high* through the gift of the Holy Spirit. The Son of God was not born in an inn, where strangers and travelers made a brief stop in their journey to some other place.

Instead, Jesus was born in the manger of the Lord. The Lord God cares for and feeds his flock. Examples of God's loving care abound in the biblical texts that foreshadow the coming of Christ, the Good Shepherd. Here are only a few: "David went back and forth from Saul to feed his father's sheep at Bethlehem" (1 Samuel 17:15); "He will feed his flock like a shepherd; / he will gather the lambs in his arms" (Isaiah 40:11a); "The wolf and the lamb shall feed together, / the lion shall eat straw like the ox" (Isaiah 65:25a); "I will give you shepherds after my own heart, who will feed you with knowledge and understanding" (Jeremiah 3:15); "I will set up over them one shepherd, my servant David, and he shall feed them: he shall feed them and be their shepherd" (Ezekiel 34:23).

What does the Lord feed his flock?

Nestled in the manger, the Shepherd King, son of David and Son of God, offers himself as a gift, completely vulnerable and helpless before his chosen flock, very much as he was at the moment when he gave himself up to be nailed to the cross. His flesh truly is food for the world. Such a gift is incomprehensible to us! Even at the moment of his birth, the rough wood of the manger foreshadows the rough wood of the cross, and the bands of cloth in which Mary so carefully wraps her child hark to the linen bands used to wrap Jesus' body for burial. These signs help us to ponder the continuity in Jesus' life; his birth at Bethlehem contains the seed of his glorious birth in the Resurrection, when the Son of God entered into his risen life, a life we also enter in Baptism, when we too are "wrapped" in a white garment. The altar is our holy manger. Each time we approach, Christ feeds us with his very life.

Prayer

You have become a new creation, and have clothed yourself in Christ.

See in this white garment the outward sign of your Christian dignity. With your family and friends to help you by word and example, bring that dignity unstained into the everlasting life of heaven.

From the Rite of Baptism for Children, 99

When holy Mother Church brought me out
of the water,
giving birth to me in Baptism,
she cared for me with
careful hands like those of Mary—
the same hands that held and clothed you!
Thank you for this garment,
for those tender hands,
and for the light I wear.
Amen.

Reading

In that region there were shepherds living in the fields, keeping watch over their flock by night. Then an angel of the Lord stood before them, and the glory of the Lord shone around them, and they were terrified.

Luke 2:8–9

Reflection

Taking care of sheep certainly seems to be the most successful way to receive a message from God! We know that Abraham kept herds, and Moses was shepherding his flock when he first heard the voice of God in the burning bush. When Jesse sent for his son David so that he could be recognized and anointed by the prophet Samuel, the unsuspecting youth was in the hills outside of Bethlehem, tending sheep.

The Lord God himself is a Shepherd who feeds and waters his own sheep, dresses their wounds, names them, knows them, and searches for them when they wander. When human shepherds undertake these same responsibilities, they can't help but participate in God's nature. Even if the shepherds in Bethlehem did not appreciate the sacred dimension of their work, their everyday duties would have slowly conformed them in the image of God. Yet we know that as Jews they were not strangers to the psalms of David and the prophesies of Isaiah and Ezekiel. These sacred shepherding texts were read and prayed so often in the synagogues that they must have given shape and substance to the shepherds' inner lives.

Whenever we serve those who are smaller, weaker, or poorer than we are, we absorb a catechism far richer than any spelled in words. Simply giving the substance of our lives to any helpless creature makes us able to understand God's own wonderful language, whose name is Absolute Love. Then when our shepherd calls us by name, we have ears to hear. And when he shows us his shining glory, we have eyes to see.

Prayer

The Lord Jesus made the deaf hear and the dumb speak.
May he soon touch your ears to receive his word,
and your mouth to proclaim his faith,
to the praise and glory of God the Father.

From the Rite of Baptism for Children, 101

Lord,
    open my eyes, that I may gaze upon you,
    open my ears that I may recognize your voice.
    Let my small song join with all the choirs in heaven
    to sing your glory forever.
    Amen.

Reading

But the angel said to them, "Do not be afraid; for see—I am bringing you good news of great joy for all the people: to you is born this day in the city of David a Savior, who is the Messiah, the Lord. This will be a sign for you; you will find a child wrapped in bands of cloth and lying in a manger."

Luke 2:10–12

Reflection

Imagine the eyes of these shepherds! Not only did they behold the heavenly host and the glory of the Lord shining around them, but they could also "see" this mysterious sign that God held up for them: a child wrapped in bands of cloth and lying in a manger.

Perhaps we have listened to this announcement so many times that our ears no longer hear how strange it is. But consider: the Mighty God, who communicates through terrifying angels and shining glory, tells the shepherds that the coming of the longed-for Messiah, the most truly marvelous, wonderful, and glorious event in the history of the cosmos, can be discerned by contemplating a child, clothed as any child and lying in an animal's feeding trough. The angel's announcement is absurd. How did the shepherds reconcile the display of terrifying glory and the promise of an ordinary child lying in an unusually humble bed?

We are slow to recognize that joy is born only out of the simplest, most unlikely things and often under the most difficult circumstances. Displays of power and glory have the power to terrify us, but only small, quiet, ordinary, and humble events are capable of giving us the joy we hunger for. And this joy, which we would take for our constant banquet if we could only grasp it, often manifests itself after a trial. The child arrives after a difficult labor.

And just as they had appeared to announce his birth, angels appeared at Jesus' Resurrection to announce to the women who visited his tomb that he had risen from the dead. The angels told the women to remember Jesus' words. With plain words, Jesus had foretold his own death and Resurrection, but at the time no one had understood him. Even to his closest friends, his words had seemed absurd.

In the scriptures, Jesus calls our attention to one perfect pearl, a tiny seed, a pinch of yeast, a grape vine; he tells us that in order to receive the kingdom of God embodied in these signs, we must be willing to sell all we own, to sacrifice the seed to the soil, to lose the yeast in the flour, to submit to the pruning shears. Jesus taught that great joy is born of things hidden in plain view, but revealed to the weak and vulnerable. He should know!

Prayer

Has not God made foolish the wisdom of the world? For since, in the wisdom of God, the world did not know God through wisdom, God decided, through the foolishness of our proclamation, to save those who believe. For Jews demand signs and Greeks desire wisdom, but we proclaim Christ crucified, a stumbling block to Jews and foolishness to Gentiles, but to those who are called, both Jews and Greeks, Christ the power of God and the wisdom of God. For God's foolishness is wiser than human wisdom, and God's weakness is stronger than human strength.

1 Corinthians 1:20b–25

God,
Let me be absurd,
if foolishness is the path to you.
Let me withstand the poor opinion
of my neighbors,
who do not know you.
O, let me be weak and small with you.
Amen.

Reading

And suddenly there was with the angel a multitude of the heavenly host, praising God and saying,
"Glory to God in the highest heaven,
and on earth peace among those whom he favors!"
When the angels had left them and gone into heaven, the shepherds said to one another, "Let us go now to Bethlehem and see this thing that has taken place, which the Lord has made known to us." So they went with haste and found Mary and Joseph, and the child lying in the manger. When they saw this, they made known what had been told them about this child; and all who heard it were amazed at what the shepherds told them. But Mary treasured all these words and pondered them in her heart.

Luke 2:13–19

Reflection

Do we treat the Incarnation as if it were a mere metaphor to be parsed? Or do we limit the Word of God by reading too literally?

Perhaps we could try a third path, the path of Saint Peter: After the women told the apostles what they had seen and heard at the empty tomb, "Peter got up and ran to the tomb; stooping and looking in, he saw the linen cloths by themselves; then he went home, amazed at what had happened" (Luke 24:12).

Peter's experience, recorded in this Gospel, is a precious gift to us. Like those who heard the shepherds' account, Peter's heart opened in amazement. We, like Peter, need to "stoop" in order to experience wonder: we need to be prepared to abandon our fixed perspective, to acknowledge our littleness before the Mystery, and to seek the small and the overlooked. Also like Peter, we need to be willing to "look in" if we wish to be astonished: only prolonged, prayerful attention will lead to amazement. Christ himself was born to the Jewish people only after centuries of attentive waiting.

After Jesus rose from the dead, he asked Peter to feed his lambs, and thus invited the fisherman to become a shepherd. Like the shepherds who brought amazement to all who heard their account, Saint Peter, through the ministry of the Church, continues to recount this amazing event to all the body of Christ. Like a shepherd, he feeds us, not with straw, but with the flesh and blood of our Savior, Christ himself.

Let us *run* to this banquet, *stoop* to contemplate our God in a thin wafer of bread and a mouthful of wine, *see* the deathless one who takes away all sin and suffering, and please God, let us go home *amazed*.

Prayer

As for me, I shall behold your face in righteousness;
    when I awake I shall be satisfied, beholding your likeness.

Psalm 17:15

earest Mary,
    You were the first to gaze
    upon the face of Christ and live.
Show us your child,
O blessed Mother of God!!
Only in the act of looking on your Son
can I awake and be satisfied.
Please, show me his face,
that I may eat and drink
and live.
Amen.

Reading

The shepherds returned, glorifying and praising God for all
they had heard and seen, as it had been told them.

Luke 2:20

Reflection

Everything the shepherds had seen and heard matched up with what
they'd been told. They had been told they would see a child, and
they did indeed see a child. He was to be wrapped in bands of cloth,
and he *was* wrapped. They were to find him in a manger, and there
he was.

They did not see a throne, or a scepter, or millions bowing and pay-
ing homage to the new king. Water didn't run uphill, the donkey
didn't begin to say, "moo." Everything was exactly as they'd been told.

We, too, have been told to look for signs: water, light, oil, bread,
and wine. These signs are promises to us. They speak of divinity
and universal peace, authority and passion, espousal and protection,
enlightenment and glory. When we enter a church, any church,
we see these signs, exactly as we've been promised.

Some might object: But no angels told us to look for these signs!

Here is where memory, that human gift par excellence, saves us
from grave danger.

One way to understand eternity is to recognize it as God's memory.
Our own imperfect memories are a means of approaching the
mystery of eternity. The distance between the function of human
memory and God's own eternal Now, provides us with a glimpse
of our littleness. In the liturgy, God transforms our memory into
his omnipresent Now, and we receive all moments of sacred history
through the Lord of history, who is embodied in a handful of
flattened wheat and a draught of ordinary wine.

And so angels *did* tell us! Not only do we visit the hill in
Bethlehem every moment that we live the Eucharist, but that hill
and those angels are present today in the voices of all the witnesses
who have listened to God in every generation. These "heavenly

messengers" form an unbroken chain that extends back to the ones who walked with Jesus in the land of Israel. We trust their memory because it forms the heart of God's eternal Now. The Incarnation has become a Church, built of living stones, a vine whose growth is supported by the cross and whose tendrils reach up to heaven.

Prayer

In memory of his death and resurrection,
we offer you, Father, this life-giving bread,
this saving cup.

From Eucharistic Prayer II

ear Lord,
I offer you this bread,
this cup.
They represent all that I am,
my own body and blood.
Take them, convert them,
sanctify them in your name.
In your memory, the crucifixion
and your glorious Resurrection
happen Now.
And so, please remember me, Lord,
when you come into your kingdom.
Amen.

The Birth of Jesus Christ
and the
Adoration of the Magi

❧

Matthew 2:1–12

Reading

In the time of King Herod, after Jesus was born in Bethlehem of Judea, magi from the East came to Jerusalem, asking, "Where is the child who has been born king of the Jews? For we have observed his star at its rising, and have come to pay him homage."

Matthew 2:1–2

Reflection

We too may ask, "Where is the child?"

As people decry the commercialism and superficiality of the Christmas holiday, they imagine that the gifts represent our offering to the Christ child; the tree reminds them of Christ's risen life, and the Christmas lights indicate the Great Light prophesied by Isaiah. God's faithful servants strive after holiness while they go about the endless preparations that mark our modern Christmas tradition. They feel frustrated because Christmas seems to come earlier and earlier every year, and still they can find so little time for prayer. Meanwhile, voices from the pulpit tell them they must wait to shop, to decorate, to turn on their lights.

In fact, two very different events coincide during our month of December. There is a secular holiday, called "Christmas," that has almost nothing to do with the birth of Jesus in Bethlehem. This holiday involves buying gifts, preparing special foods, decorating, and putting up an evergreen tree. The whole month of December is given over to this winter festival. Meanwhile, there is the real Christmas, anticipated during the month of December but celebrated now, even as the curbs in our neighborhoods are lined with broken pine trees awaiting the mulch machine. This other Christmas is quieter, hidden behind the winking lights and torn wrapping paper. In early December, while the first Christmas brought its noisy warmth and cheer, the true Christmas, with its never-ending burst of holy joy, was momentarily concealed beneath purple cloth and solemn chants.

But the commercial Christmas itself hungers for more than can be supplied by warmth and cheer alone. It hops from party to party, exhausting itself in excesses until it collapses on New Year's Day with a false promise to do better on its tuneless lips.

But for the watchful ones, nothing has ended! For us the child has only just been born. We await his first steps, his first words, his flowering into an adult. In Christ, even now, we are always beginning anew. We make no resolutions. We merely remain with our hands open, contemplating the Gift that grows in wonder, through no effort of our own.

Prayer

Where can I go from your spirit?
  Or where can I flee from your presence?
If I ascend to heaven, you are there;
  if I make my bed in Sheol, you are there.
If I take the wings of the morning
  and settle at the farthest limits of the sea,
even there your hand shall lead me,
  and your right hand shall hold me fast

Psalm 139:7–10

ivine Child,
    Even in the commercial Christmas,
    you are present. Your holy light
  eclipses all false promises
  and leads those who will honor
  their deepest hunger
  to the farthest limits of the sea,
  to your door.
  Amen.

Reading

When King Herod heard this, he was frightened, and all Jerusalem with him; and calling together all the chief priests and scribes of the people, he inquired of them where the Messiah was to be born.

Matthew 2:3–4

Reflection

The magi seek the King of the Jews. Even before they have met him, they recognize his royalty and dominion. Another thirty-three years will pass before Jesus publicly assumes this title and ascends his one earthly throne, when, beneath a sign that reads *The King of the Jews,* he dies on the cross.

How are the magi able to see and recognize his star, and how do they know its significance, when Jerusalem, upon hearing of this new star, grows frightened and has to consult with specialists in order to know what is written in its scrolls?

Prayer

I see him, but not now;
   I behold him, but not near—
a star shall come out of Jacob,
   and a scepter shall rise out of Israel.

Numbers 24:17a

Star of the morning,
I see you now. You are near!
In your light I see
Light beyond all telling.
Please let me always turn my gaze to heaven
so that when you rise with each new day,
I won't miss you.
Amen.

Reading

They told him, "In Bethlehem of Judea; for so it has been written by the prophet:

> 'And you, Bethlehem, in the land of Judah,
>   are by no means least among the rulers of Judah;
> for from you shall come a ruler
>   who is to shepherd my people Israel.' "

Matthew 2:5–6

Reflection

The message of the prophets might be summed up in two words: "Expect miracles!"

We are living the holy season of Christmas, when the great miracle of the Incarnation makes us attentive to the miraculous gifts of God's first creation. Christ's birth as a child in Bethlehem opens our eyes to the meaning and purpose of history. Even in mid-winter, we welcome the Light. Even with the earth quiet and buried in snow, we go out to meet Life. For those with eyes to see, prophesies are being fulfilled each and every day!

Yet, a tension exists between the expectation that characterizes our Advent observation and the celebration of Christmas. Even as, in the present moment, we live the fullness of the Christmas miracle, the gift of the Incarnation will elude us if we completely abandon our practice of Advent anticipation. The Incarnation of Jesus Christ is an event that encompasses *all* of history, both the waiting and the Parousia. Thus, to encounter the living Christ is to experience joyful hope and intense gratitude at one and the same time. To live in *perpetual* hope would be to deny that God has answered our every need and has given us more than we could have ever asked for; and to stop expecting Christ would mean measuring God's gifts with a human yardstick.

Prayer

As it is written,
> "What no eye has seen, nor ear heard,
> nor the human heart conceived,
> what God has prepared for those who love him."

1 Corinthians 2:9

O y Good Shepherd,
You lead me to the clearest water,
to the greenest pastures,
to a table set with joy
that you have prepared for me.
I am filled with wonder,
thinking about what you will
bring next.
Amen.

Reading

Then Herod secretly called for the wise men and learned from them the exact time when the star had appeared. Then he sent them to Bethlehem, saying, "Go and search diligently for the child; and when you have found him, bring me word so that I may also go and pay him homage."

Matthew 2:7–8

Reflection

At the time of Moses, the wicked king Balak summoned a man named Balaam from the East, requiring that Balaam place a curse on the Israelites. Ancient sources refer to Balaam as a *magos*. Instead of cursing the Israelites, Balaam blessed them and prophesied that a star would rise out of Jacob (Numbers 24:17).

And now in Jerusalem three more magi come from the East with news of a star. Another wicked king plots to destroy the hope of Israel. If, instead of asking where the Messiah was to be born, Herod had asked his advisors to explain the meaning of this new star, he might have heard the prophesy of Balaam and seen himself in Balak, as in a mirror.

Biblical history doesn't repeat itself; rather, certain moments of heightened intensity point ahead to moments of even greater glory. Each time a theme resurfaces in salvation history, God reveals more details of his cosmic plan, and the total picture comes into better focus. But the evil that exists in the world does not change. Each time it expresses itself in history, it is nauseatingly identical: darkness is always just dark, but light gathers luminosity and shines more brightly in each succeeding generation.

Balak and Herod are expressions of the same absence. Herod, like Balak, cannot adapt to new circumstances because there can be no such thing as a new and creative expression of nothingness; dead things don't change.

But compare Balaam's star to the star of the magi! The first star is a promise, while the second is an indication of fulfillment. The first star was gleaned by one holy man, the second shone in the sky for all to see. Balaam's star symbolized victory for the Israelites' army, but the star of the magi pointed to Christ, who conquers sin and death.

Prayer

The sun shall no longer be
   your light by day,
nor for brightness shall the moon
   give light to you by night;
but the LORD will be your everlasting light,
   and your God will be your glory.
Your sun shall no more go down,
   or your moon withdraw itself;
for the LORD will be your everlasting light,
   and your days of mourning shall be ended.

Isaiah 60:19–20

ne day, O Light of all the nations,
   your light will overpower the sun and moon,
   and the heavens themselves will reflect
your total splendor.
Let me be there, on that day, O Lord!
Amen.

Reading

When they had heard the king, they set out; and there, ahead of them, went the star that they had seen at its rising, until it stopped over the place where the child was.

Matthew 2:9

Reflection

To the shepherds, God sends angels who give instructions that will lead them to the Child. The magi, on the other hand, observe a star; though mute, this star moves, pointing out the location of the Holy Family. How do we account for the two very different ways that God announces the birth of Jesus in the Gospels?

So many paths lead to Christ! Scholars encounter him in theology, cantors experience him in sacred music, catechists meet him in the children they serve. And consider all the religious orders! In fact, each person receives a unique and particular life, given for the purpose of meeting and following Christ. Within our concrete experiences, the Good Shepherd calls us in our own individual languages. The Voice that one recognizes may not carry the same inflection as the Voice another recognizes. And yet, there is only one Shepherd who speaks to all. He wishes to meet us where we are. He loves us, *as we are.*

The sheep of the Good Shepherd do not require a fancy education, or a lengthy period of initiation, or a course in a foreign language to recognize his voice! They only need to *pay attention.* In fact, training and preparation sometimes make it more difficult to hear his call. Consider: who does Jesus place before us to serve as a model of discipleship? *A small child.* Though many have yet to discover it, Christ has always known quite well that children age three, and even younger, will respond with spontaneous joy and awe to sacred realities that often sound either routine or esoteric to adults.

The angels and the star each announce the Incarnation. Through the Gospels, both celestial messengers proclaim the Good News of great joy to us now, where we are, today. Yet, for us there is more.

We ourselves see the living Christ in light, touch and see him in water and oil, and taste him in bread and wine. Through these sacramental gifts, he transforms us, along with our brothers and sisters, so that we encounter him in one another, as well. Christ is alive in every detail of our lives!

Prayer

Now there were devout Jews from every nation under heaven living in Jerusalem. And at this sound the crowd gathered and was bewildered, because each one heard them speaking in the native language of each.

Acts of the Apostles 2:5–6

Good Shepherd,
You speak to me in my native tongue.
You use my given name!
How blessed I am
to hear your voice,
to taste your joy,
to see your face,
and live.
Amen.

Reading

When they saw that the star had stopped, they were over-whelmed with joy.

Matthew 2:10

Reflection

We stand at a threshold, and we know very well what waits for us behind the door.

The magi had come a long way, and now what stood before their eyes? An ordinary door to an ordinary house situated in an ordinary town. Yet now they knew that their exhausting journey was over. With unshakeable conviction, they understood that their heart's desire was within reach, that every promise would be kept and every prayer answered. In a flash, one fact had communicated all these things and more. *They saw that the star had stopped.*

Do we know what we have found when we stand in front of the Eucharistic table?

Truly, we stand at a threshold, and we know very well what waits for us behind the door.

Prayer

Long may he live!
  May gold of Sheba be given to him.
May prayer be made for him continually,
  and blessings invoked for him all day long.
May there be abundance of grain in the land;
  may it wave on the tops of the mountains;
  may its fruit be like Lebanon;
and may people blossom in the cities
  like the grass of the field.
May his name endure forever,
  his fame continue as long as the sun.
May all nations be blessed in him;
  may they pronounce him happy.
Blessed be the LORD, the God of Israel,
  who alone does wondrous things.
Blessed be his glorious name forever;
  may his glory fill the whole earth. Amen and Amen.

Psalm 72:15–19

earest Christ in the Holy Eucharist,
Even before I behold you,
I am filled with joy
  when you are near.
  When I forget, or doubt,
  let me hear your voice again;
  remind me that
  this day I will be with you in paradise.
  Amen.

Reading

On entering the house, they saw the child with Mary his mother; and they knelt down and paid him homage. Then, opening their treasure chests, they offered him gifts of gold, frankincense, and myrrh. And having been warned in a dream not to return to Herod, they left for their own country by another road.

Matthew 2:11–12

Reflection

First, the magi experience joy, then immediately they express reverence and offer gifts to Christ. Joy is inseparable from reverence and offering.

Without joy, reverence is merely an empty gesture made out of fear, or worse: a mockery. And offering without joy is a commercial transaction, always secretly hoping for repayment. But joy, without reverence and offering, is an absurdity, impossible even to imagine!

Only a view with no horizon, an "overflowing cup," inspires joy. We glimpse a reality that is endless, plunge ourselves into a mystery with no final definition, no limit. Because joy is only wakened when we find ourselves face to face with the Infinite, reverence, that recognition that we stand so small before Eternity, always accompanies joy.

And quite spontaneously, we *know* that the only way to prolong this holy experience is to offer ourselves. We offer ourselves almost reflexively, having arrived at this knowledge through divine inspiration and not through any intellectual process. Yet upon reflection, the intellect confirms that when we offer ourselves, we participate in God's essential nature. The Good Shepherd gives the sheep all they need, even to the point of laying down his own life. In fact, without his prior gift, we would be incapable of giving anything. But through him, with him, and in him, we do give ourselves, along with all the gifts he has ever given to us, and in this way, we prolong our joy and enter more profoundly into relationship with the Author of all joy.

Prayer

Then you shall see and be radiant;
   your heart shall thrill and rejoice,
because the abundance of the sea shall be brought to you,
   the wealth of the nations shall come to you.
They shall bring gold and frankincense,
   and shall proclaim the praise of the LORD.

Isaiah 60:5, 6b

ear Christ,
   If I had gold and frankincense,
   I would give them to you.
My words and thoughts and dreams
are my gold.
Enthusiasm and passion
are my frankincense.
Love is my myrrh.
Take all these things
and more.
With you,
I have all I need.
Amen.

Bibliography

1. Albright, W. F., and C. S. Mann. *Matthew*. (The Anchor Bible, Doubleday and Company, Inc., 1971).
2. Brown, Raymond E. *An Introduction to the New Testament*. (The Anchor Bible Reference Library, Doubleday and Company, Inc., 1997).
3. Cavalletti, Sofia. *The Religious Potential of the Child*. (Archdiocese of Chicago: Liturgy Training Publications, 1992).
4. Cavalletti, Sofia. *The Religious Potential of the Child ages 6 to 12 Years Old*. (Archdiocese of Chicago: Liturgy Training Publications, 2002).
5. Cavalletti, Sofia. *History's Golden Thread*. (Archdiocese of Chicago: Liturgy Training Publications, 1999).
6. Cavalletti, Sofia. *Living Liturgy*. (Archdiocese of Chicago: Liturgy Training Publications, 1998).
7. Cavalletti, et al. *The Good Shepherd and the Child, A Joyful Journey*. (Archdiocese of Chicago: Liturgy Training Publications, 1996).
8. Danielou, Jean. *Prayer, The Mission of the Church*. (William B. Eerdmans Publishing Company, 1996).
9. Fitzmyer, Joseph A. *The Gospel According to Luke I-IX*. (The Anchor Bible, Doubleday and Company, Inc., 1970).
10. Giussani, Luigi. *The Religious Sense*. (McGill Queens's, 1997).
11. Giussani, Luigi. *At the Origin of the Christian Claim,* (McGill Queens's, 1998).
12. Giussani, Luigi. *Why the Church?* (McGill Queens's, 2000).
13. Gobbi, Gianna. *Listening to God with Children*. (Treehaus Communications, Inc., 1998).
14. Guardini, Romano. *Preparing Yourself for Mass*. (Sofia Institute Press, 1997).
15. Hahn, Scott, and Curtis Mitch. *Ignatius Catholic Study Bible, The Gospel of Luke*. (Ignatius Press, 2001).
16. Hahn, Scott, and Curtis Mitch. *Ignatius Catholic Study Bible, The Gospel of Matthew*. (Ignatius Press, 2000).
17. Houselander, Caryll. *The Reed of God*. (Sheed and Ward, Ltd., 1944).
18. Lillig, Tina, ed. *Essential Realities*. (Archdiocese of Chicago: Liturgy Training Publications, 2004).
19. Montessori, Maria. *The Child in the Church*. (Catechetical Guild Educational Society, 1965).
20. *The Collected Journals of the Catechesis of the Good Shepherd,* vol. 1 and 2. (Archdiocese of Chicago: Liturgy Training Publications, 1998 and 2003).
21. McReynolds, Paul R. *Word Study Greek-English New Testament*. (Tyndale House Publishers, Inc., 1998).

The Catechesis of the Good Shepherd

The Catechesis of the Good Shepherd was begun in Rome over fifty years ago by Sofia Cavalletti and her Montessori collaborator, Gianna Gobbi. Today the Catechesis can be found in nineteen countries around the world.

This approach to religious formation offers an opportunity for adults and children to share their faith life together. They meet in a specially prepared room called the atrium, the ancient name of the place near the church where early Christians prepared to enter more fully into the community of faith.

In this atrium the children use simple, beautiful materials to meditate on the scriptures, the liturgy, and the sacraments. Order, repetition, and movement are some of the principles that allow the children to make both liturgical and scriptural components of our faith a part of their everyday life.

Quietly pondering the infancy narratives, kingdom parables, geography of the holy land, and elements from liturgy can nurture the child's knowledge and love of God. It is the meeting of the mystery of God and the mystery of the child that gives the Catechesis of the Good Shepherd its life.

More information about the Catechesis of the Good Shepherd can be found on the Internet at www.cgsusa.org.